PROCLAMATIONS for LIFE

*CHANGING YOUR LIFE
BY DECLARING GOD'S WORD*

Copyright © 2014 by Dr. Peter D. Wyns
Great Reward Publishing
PO Box 36324
Rock Hill, SC 29732

www.peterwyns.com
email: ReachUs@peterwyns.com

All Scriptures used are taken from the New International Version. Scriptures taken from the Holy Bible, New International Version® Copyright © 1973, 1978, 1984 by International Bible Society.

All rights reserved. No part of this publication may be reproduced without written permission of Great Reward Publishing

Cover Design by: Judy Wilson

Page Design by: Toelke Associates

Editing by: Rev. Jesse Enns

First Great Reward Publishing edition published 2014.

Manufactured in the United States of America by Versa Press Inc.

PROCLAMATIONS for LIFE

*CHANGING YOUR LIFE
BY DECLARING GOD'S WORD*

BY DR. PETER WYNS

Great Reward Publishing

About the Author

Dr. Peter Wyns comes from a family of preachers and Bible teachers. Both sets of grandparents were missionaries and his father and four of his brothers are ministers. Dr. Wyns has pastored local churches for over forty years, planted new churches and ministered in more than thirty-five nations around the world.

He was co-founder and director of Intercessors for Canada for eighteen years and was the chairman of the National Prayer Committee of Canada. He is the president and founder of Christians for Messiah Ministries and the Senior Pastor of Antioch International Church. Dr. Wyns is an accomplished author and is currently sought out as an international Bible speaker. He speaks at conferences, church meetings, Bible schools and leadership training seminars throughout the USA and abroad. He ministers on a wide variety of Bible themes.

Other titles by Dr. Peter Wyns include:

Fighting Death
Unexpected Fire: A Powerful New Study on the Book of Revelation
Israel's Coming Revival
Blessings or Curses for the Next Generation
Chronicles of Righteousness — volumes 1 & 2
Great Reward for Kids — volumes 1 & 2

◦ Dedications ◦

I dedicate this book to my friends and coworkers at Antioch International Church and to all who partner with us through Christians for Messiah Ministries. This has been a year of amazing new beginnings and all have been stretched to facilitate growth and the call of God.

I have been blessed and encouraged to have such friends and a church family of faith. They have sacrificed extensively, walked in the joy of the Lord and risen to the task at hand. I can think of no finer people than those whom God has joined to us for this season. Together, by His grace, we will march forward to fulfill the word of the Lord in our time.

Introduction

Veterans of the faith know the power of the spoken word. They understand that our present situation and our future are largely determined by what we speak. Whether it is an idle word, or an intended one, everything we say has a consequence. The word of God spoken in faith will not return unto Him without accomplishing its mission. In the same way, every negative or evil suggestion can open doors of darkness. All of us should be careful about what we say. It is not good enough for us to keep our tongue from speaking evil; we should train our lips to proclaim that which is good.

Proclamations for Life is a manual of biblical declarations. They are intended to be spoken out loud with confidence and faith. Within the book, there are 52 proclamations — one for each week of the year. Scriptures have been added on the overleaf of each page, to reinforce the importance of speaking forth the word of God.

I encourage you to keep this book with you as you travel, as well as in your home. Repeat one declaration every day, for the entire week, and let it soak into the atmosphere around you. Do not lay the word of God down but let it be a light unto your feet and a lamp unto your path. I pronounce the blessings of God over all who speak forth the words of this book. I speak it over you in Jesus' name.

Many blessings,
Peter Wyns

Proclamations for Life

Psalm 35:28

My tongue will proclaim Your righteousness,
Your praises all day long.

Week One

We are anxious for nothing,
but in everything by prayer and supplication,
with thanksgiving, we make our requests known to God.

We receive the peace of God which passes understanding.
The peace of God guards our hearts and minds because,
every day, we put our trust in Jesus.

We rule our thoughts. That means, whatever things
are true, whatever things are noble, whatever things
are just, whatever things are lovely, whatever things
are of good report, we think on these things.

ADAPTATION OF PHILIPPIANS 4:6–8

Psalm 29:9

The voice of the LORD twists the oaks
and strips the forests bare.
And in His temple all cry, "Glory!"

Week Two

We have come to Jesus, the Living Stone.
We are also living stones. We have become
a spiritual house, to be a holy priesthood
offering spiritual sacrifices to God.

We are a chosen people, a royal priesthood,
a holy nation, a people belonging to God.

We proclaim the praises of Him who called us out of
darkness into His wonderful light. Once we were not a
people, but now we are the people of God; once we had
not received mercy, but now we have received mercy.

ADAPTATION OF 1 PETER 2:4–10

James 1:21

Therefore, get rid of all moral filth and the evil that is so prevalent and humbly accept the word planted in you, which can save you.

◈ Week Three ◈

In all things God works for the good of those who love Him,
who have been called according to His purpose.
Who can bring any charge against us whom God
has chosen? It is God who justifies.

Nothing can separate us from the love of God in Christ
Jesus: Not death, nor life, neither angels nor demons,
neither the present, nor the future, nor any powers,
not height nor depth, nor anything else in all creation
will be able to separate us from the love of God
that is in Christ Jesus our Lord.

ADAPTATION OF ROMANS 8:28–39

Psalm 45:1

My heart is stirred by a noble theme
as I recite my verses for the King;
my tongue is the pen of a skillful writer

Week Four

In the beginning was the Word, and the Word
was with God, and the Word was God. He is Jesus Christ.
He was in the beginning. He is the beginning and the end.

Through Him all things were made; without Him nothing
was made that has been made. He also made me and my
family. I am fearfully and wonderfully made in God's image.

In Him was life, and that life was the light of men.
The light shines in the darkness. My family and I need Jesus.
I welcome Jesus into my life, my home and my family.
He is the source of life therefore, we will serve the Lord.

ADAPTATION OF JOHN 1:1–5

Psalm 49:3

My mouth will speak words of wisdom;
the meditation of my heart will give you understanding.

∞ **Week Five** ∞

I declare that God really takes care of me and my family.
The Lord is my shepherd, I shall not want. He makes me
lie down in green pastures, He leads me beside
quiet waters, He restores my soul.

He guides me in paths of righteousness for His name's sake.
Even though I walk through the valley of the shadow of
death, I will fear no evil, for You are with me,
Your rod and your staff, comfort me.

You prepare a table before me in the presence of my enemies.
You anoint my head with oil, my cup overflows.
Surely goodness and love will follow me all
the days of my life. I and my family will
dwell in the house of the Lord forever.

ADAPTATION OF PSALM 23

Psalm 119:72

The law from Your mouth is more precious to me
than thousands of pieces of silver and gold

∽ Week Six ∾

By God's grace, we throw off everything that hinders our
spiritual progress. We remove the sin that entangles us, and
we run with perseverance, the race that is set before us.

We fix our eyes on Jesus because He is the author
and the finisher of our faith. We consider Jesus
who endured the cross and we look to Him
so we do not grow weary or lose heart.

We do not make light of the Lord's discipline when He
rebukes us because we know He loves us and is treating us
as His children. We endure hardship because we know it
produces a harvest of righteousness and peace. Therefore we
strengthen our feeble arms and our weak knees and we walk
on level paths so that we may be continuously healed.

ADAPTATION OF HEBREWS 12: 1–13

Psalm 145:21

My mouth will speak in praise of the LORD.
Let every creature praise His holy name
for ever and ever

Week Seven

I constantly remember the Lord, therefore I have hope.
I know the Lord spreads His love over me. That is why I am
not consumed. His compassions over me never fail.
They are new every morning.
Great is your faithfulness to me, oh Lord!

I say to myself, "The Lord is my portion; therefore I will
wait for Him. The Lord is always good to those
who wait for Him; to the one who seeks Him,
He is faithful. I will seek you, oh Lord!"
I will wait quietly for the salvation of the Lord.

Lord, you hear my voice when I call.
My heart says, "Seek His face." So, your face, oh Lord,
I will seek. I will see your goodness Lord.
I will wait for you; I will be strong and take heart!

ADAPTATION OF LAMENTATIONS 3:22–27,
PSALM 27:7–8,14

Isaiah 50:4

The Sovereign LORD has given me a well-instructed tongue,
to know the word that sustains the weary.
He wakens me morning by morning,
wakens my ear to listen like one being instructed.

◈ Week Eight ◈

I am strong in the Lord, because I stand under the covering
of His mighty power. God has given me authority, so I push
back the plans of the devil, and claim my victory!

I fight against the darkness of this world, and I battle
against the evil power of the heavenly realms.
That is why I put on the whole armor of God.
When the devil attacks, I stand firm.

I have the belt of truth around my waist. I wear the
breastplate of God's righteousness. My feet are shod
with the gospel of peace and I put on the helmet of salvation.
I take up the shield of faith and the sword of the Spirit,
which is the word of God with all prayer.
I am ready to fight. With God's anointing, I will win.

ADAPTATION OF EPHESIANS 6:10–18

1 Corinthians 2:7

We declare God's wisdom, a mystery that has been hidden and that God destined for our glory before time began.

Week Nine

Do you not know? Have you not heard?
The Lord is the everlasting God, the Creator of the
ends of the earth. He will not become tired
and no one has an understanding like He does.

The Lord gives strength to the weary, and increases
the power of the weak. Even youths grow tired
and stumble and fall, but those who wait on the Lord
are renewed by His amazing power.

Those who wait on the Lord will renew their strength.
They will rise up with wings like eagles; they will run and
not grow weary, they will walk and not faint. I have put my
trust completely in the Lord, therefore I always rise up
with eagle's wings, I run without growing weary,
and I keep walking in the strength of the Lord.

ADAPTATION OF ISAIAH 40:28–31

1 Peter 4:11

If anyone speaks, they should do so as one who speaks the very words of God.

Week Ten

The teachings of Jesus are working in my life;
that is why I am blessed. As a disciple, I live as one who is
poor in spirit so that I may receive the kingdom of Heaven.
As I mourn He comforts me.

By God's grace, I become meek; and with that attitude,
I inherit the earth. I hunger and thirst for His righteousness,
and He fills me. I show mercy to others and
Jesus continues to show mercy to me.

I keep my heart pure so that I may see God.
I am a peacemaker and not a troublemaker and God calls
me His child. If I am persecuted for righteousness' sake,
or for the name of Jesus, I will not waver.
I will be glad and rejoice because my reward is great.

ADAPTATION OF MATTHEW 5:3–12

Deuteronomy 6:6-7

These commandments that I give you today are
to be on your hearts. Impress them on your children.
Talk about them when you sit at home and when you walk
along the road, when you lie down and when you get up.

Week Eleven

With all the inhabitants of the earth,
I shout for Joy to the Lord. I worship Him with gladness.
I come before Him with joyful singing and a merry heart.
Lord, you have my allegiance.

I know that the Lord is God. It is He who has made us
and not we ourselves; therefore I belong to Jesus.
We are His people, the sheep of His pasture.
I enter His gates with thanksgiving.
I enter His courts with praise. I come to bless the Lord.

I give thanks to you Lord, I praise your name.
Jesus, you are good; your love endures forever;
your faithfulness is for all generations. I receive
your covering over my life and over my family, forever.

ADAPTATION OF PSALM 100

Proverbs 18:21

The tongue has the power of life and death,
and those who love it will eat its fruit.

Week Twelve

God has blessed me, so I live by His word.
I do not walk in the counsel of the wicked or live a sinful
lifestyle. I and my family are blessed because
we do not participate in gossip or mockery.

My delight is in the Lord Jesus.
I meditate on His word day and night.
Therefore, I am like a tree planted by streams of living water.
The word of the God keeps me strong and it
makes my life fruitful. The power of the Holy Spirit
is in me and that is why I endure.

Lord, you promise to care for the wellbeing of the righteous.
You watch over me and my family. Jesus you are my all in all.
You are my wisdom, righteousness and power.
I live to worship you.

ADAPTATION OF PSALM 1

1 Peter 1:23

For you have been born again, not of perishable seed,
but of imperishable, through the living
and enduring word of God.

Week Thirteen

I Give Thanks to the Lord, for He is good.
His love endures forever. Jesus redeemed me
from the hand of the devil. I called to my God
and He saved me from my distress.

The Lord sent His word and healed me.
I thank Him for His unfailing love and wonderful deeds.
I will gladly tell of His works.

Lord, you bring pools of water to the desert.
You turn parched ground into flowing streams.
You bring the hungry to life and prepare a city for your
people. You bring the needy out of affliction and silence the
wicked. I see it and rejoice. Great is your love, oh Lord.

ADAPTATION OF PSALM 107

Romans 14:11

'As surely as I live,' says the Lord,
'every knee will bow before Me;
every tongue will acknowledge God'

Week Fourteen

I join God's chosen fast.
It loosens the chains of injustice and breaks off oppression.
I share my food with the hungry and give shelter to the poor.
I clothe the needy and help my own family.

That is why my light breaks forth like the dawn,
and my healing comes quickly. The righteousness of Jesus
goes before me and the Lord is my rear guard.
I call upon Him and He answers me.

The Lord has made me a well-watered garden, a spring
whose waters never fail. So I rebuild the ancient ruins,
I repair broken walls and restore streets to dwell in.
I work hard and then I rest in His Sabbath. That means
I lay my cares before Him. My trust is in the Lord.

ADAPTATION OF ISAIAH 58

Psalm 119:11

I have hidden Your word in my heart
that I might not sin against You.

Week Fifteen

I walk in obedience before the Lord. I keep His
commandments because I know that the Lord sets
His people on high, above all other peoples of the earth.
Jesus blesses me and my family.

I am blessed in the city, I am blessed in the country.
My children are blessed and my economy is blessed.
All that I put my hands to is blessed. When enemies come at
me from one direction, they flee in seven directions.
The Lord has established me; He watches over me.

The Lord causes me to prosper.
He makes me the head and not the tail.
That is why I will always be at the top and never
at the bottom. I am blessed in every way
because I am careful to obey the Lord.

ADAPTATION OF DEUTERONOMY 28: 1–14

James 3:5

Likewise, the tongue is a small part
of the body, but it makes great boasts.
Consider what a great forest
is set on fire by a small spark.

Week Sixteen

I am eager to tell others about Jesus. I am not ashamed of
the gospel because it is the power of God for the salvation of
everyone who believes. It is good news for all people.

In the gospel, the righteousness from God is revealed.
It is a righteousness that comes only by faith.
For it is written in the scriptures,
"The righteous will live by faith".

Like all who believe, I have been set apart for
the gospel of Jesus. The Lord gave me faith.
He has also given me grace to call others
to make Jesus the Lord of their lives.

ADAPTATION OF ROMANS 1

Ezekiel 37:9

Then he said to me, "Prophesy to the breath; prophesy, son of man, and say to it, 'This is what the Sovereign LORD says: Come, breath, from the four winds and breathe into these slain, that they may live.'"

Week Seventeen

Praise be to the name of God forever and ever;
wisdom and power are his. He changes times and seasons;
he sets up kings and deposes them.

My God gives wisdom to the wise and knowledge to the
discerning. He reveals deep and hidden things; he knows
what dwells in darkness and light dwells in him.

I thank and praise you O God.
You have given me wisdom and power.
You have made known to me your amazing love
and your great purpose. I only worship you.

ADAPTATION OF DANIEL 2:20–23

Psalm 119:16

I delight in Your decrees;
I will not neglect Your word

❦ Week Eighteen ❦

I rejoice because my life is in Christ. I am a new creation.
The old person that I was has gone and the new has come.
God reconciled me to Himself, through the blood of Jesus.

God has also given me the ministry of reconciliation.
He is reconciling the whole world to Himself
and I have become His ambassador.
We do not count men's sins against them
but lead them to forgiveness that is only found in Christ.

God made Jesus who had no sin to become sin,
so that we might become the righteousness of God in Him.

ADAPTATION OF 2 CORINTHIANS 5:17–21

Philippians 2:11

And every tongue acknowledge that Jesus Christ is Lord,
to the glory of God the Father.

Week Nineteen

O Lord, you know me.
You know when I sit down and when I rise up;
you know my thoughts. You are familiar with all my ways.
Before I speak a word, you know all of it.

You have laid your hand upon me. Where can I go from
your presence? If I go to the heavens or even to the depths,
you are there. If I settle on the far side of the sea, even there
your hand will guide me and you will hold me fast.

You created my inmost being in my mother's womb.

I am fearfully and wonderfully made and I know it very well.

ADAPTATION OF PSALM 139:1–14

Joel 2:28

I will pour out my Spirit on all people.
Your sons and daughters will prophesy,
   your old men will dream dreams,
   your young men will see visions.

Week Twenty

God makes the righteous to flourish.
He has dominion from sea to sea and from the River
to the ends of the earth. All kings will bow before Him;
all nations will serve Him.

He delivers the needy and the poor person who has no
helper. He saves and redeems them from all oppression.

Blessed be the Lord God, the God of Israel, who only does
wondrous things! Blessed be His glorious name forever!
All nations shall bow and be blessed by Him.
Let the whole earth be filled with His glory,
Amen and Amen and Amen!

ADAPTATION OF PSALM 72

Amos 3:8

The lion has roared —
who will not fear?
The Sovereign LORD has spoken —
who can but prophesy?

❧ Week Twenty-one ❧

The earth is the Lord's, and everything in it. The world
is His and all belong to Him. He founded it upon the seas
and He established it. Before time, Jesus made it all.

Who may ascend the hill of the Lord, and stand in his holy
place? He who has clean hands and a pure heart, who does
not worship idols or lie. He will be blessed by God.

I am part of the generation who seek him.
I lift my head.
I am a gateway. The King of Glory has come in
and lifted me up. Jesus is mighty in battle,
He is the King of Glory.

ADAPTATION OF PSALM 24

Psalm 119:89

Your word, LORD, is eternal;
it stands firm in the heavens.

⁘ Week Twenty-two ⁘

Lord, you have been our dwelling place throughout
all generations. Before the mountains were born or you
brought forth the earth, from everlasting you are God.

A thousand years in your sight are like a day.
Teach us to number our days that we might gain
a heart of wisdom, for we, your servants,
have received your compassion.

We are satisfied every morning with your unfailing love.
Every day, we sing for joy for your favor rests upon us. We
see your splendor and you establish the work of our hands.

ADAPTATION OF PSALM 90

2 Samuel 23:2

The Spirit of the LORD spoke through me;
His word was on my tongue.

Week Twenty-three

I have been raised with Christ, so my heart's desire is set on things above, where Christ is seated at God's right hand.

I set my mind on things above, not on earthly desires or things; for I am dead and my life is hid with Christ in God. And when Christ appears, I will appear with Him in glory.

I have put on the new self, which is being renewed into the image of Christ. I clothe myself with compassion, kindness, humility, gentleness, and patience. I forgive others and love them in order to be joined to God's people in perfect unity.

ADAPTATION OF COLOSSIANS 3

Psalm 35:28

My tongue will proclaim Your righteousness,
Your praises all day long.

Week Twenty-four

I have learned, in whatsoever state I am, to be content.
The Lord is teaching me how to find His grace and peace,
when I abound, and also when I am in lack.

I can do all things through Christ who strengthens me.
He shows me how to bless others so that I will be a sweet
aroma and an acceptable sacrifice, well pleasing to God.

My God shall supply all of my needs according to
His riches in glory by Christ Jesus. So, I live my life
to bring glory to Him, and to His Son, Jesus Christ.

ADAPTATION OF PHILIPPIANS 4:11–20

Psalm 119:105

Your word is a lamp for my feet,
a light on my path.

Week Twenty-five

I will trust in the Lord with all of my heart. I will not lean on my own understanding. In all of my ways I will acknowledge Him and He will make my paths straight.

I will not be wise in my own eyes. I will fear the Lord and turn away from evil. This brings health to my body and nourishment to my bones.

I honor the Lord with my money. I give of the first fruits of my earnings. That is why my barns will be full and why I will not fear disaster. The Lord has become my confidence.

ADAPTATION OF PROVERBS 3

Matthew 4:4

Man shall not live on bread alone,
but on every word that comes from the mouth of God.

Week Twenty-six

I make every effort to keep the unity of the Spirit, in the bond of peace. I walk humbly and I am gentle and patient. I work with my brothers and sisters in a Spirit of love.

This is the only way, because there is just one body and one Holy Spirit. All of us have one hope; the hope of eternal life, and we obtain it only through one Lord Jesus.

There is one faith; Christianity. There is one baptism. It is an ever-deepening immersion into the life of Christ. Finally, we have one Heavenly Father and He is over everything.

ADAPTATION OF EPHESIANS 4:2–6

Isaiah 55:11

So is My word that goes out from My mouth:
It will not return to Me empty,
but will accomplish what I desire
and achieve the purpose for which I sent it.

Week Twenty-seven

My soul glorifies the Lord and my spirit rejoices
in God my Savior, for he has been mindful of my humble
state. The Mighty One has done great things for me,
holy is His name.

His mercy extends to those who fear him, from generation
to generation. He has performed mighty deeds with his arm;
He has scattered those who are proud. He has brought down
rulers from their thrones, but has lifted up the humble.

He has filled the hungry with good things,
but the rich, he has sent away empty.
He helps Israel by showing his mercy.

ADAPTATION OF LUKE 1:46–54

Isaiah 40:8

The grass withers and the flowers fall,
but the word of our God endures forever.

Week Twenty-eight

I will call upon the Lord for He is worthy to be praised,
so shall I be saved from my enemies. The Lord is my rock,
my fortress and my deliverer. I take refuge in Him.

The Lord is my shield and the power of my salvation.
He is my stronghold. In my distress I call to the Lord
and He hears me from His holy temple.
All praise be to the Rock.

He parts the heavens and comes down.
He mounts the cherubim and soars on the wind.
He reaches down from on high; He takes hold of me
and draws me out of deep water.

ADAPTATION OF PSALM 18:1–17

Psalm 119:160

All Your words are true;
all Your righteous laws are eternal.

Week Twenty-nine

The Lord calls to all who are thirsty. Those who have no money can buy. The Lord makes a covenant with all who seek Him. Come while He may be found for God is near.

Let the wicked forsake his way; let him turn to the Lord and God will pardon him. God's ways are higher than ours.

God's word does not return empty; it accomplishes its purpose. Therefore, I go out with joy and I am led forth in peace. The mountains and hills break forth into song before me and the trees of the field clap their hands.

ADAPTATION OF ISAIAH 55:1–12

Psalm 107:20

He sent out His word and healed them;
He rescued them from the grave.

Week Thirty

We are not ignorant of the mystery; all Israel will be saved. Jesus, the deliverer, will come from Zion and wash their sins away. For this is the covenant He has made with them.

The gifts and calling of God, for Israel, are irrevocable.
Oh, the depth of the riches of the wisdom
and knowledge of God. How unsearchable are His
judgments and His ways are past finding out!
For God will have mercy on them all.

For from Him and through Him and to Him are all things.
So we pray for the peace of Jerusalem.
To God be the glory!

ADAPTATION OF ROMANS 11:25–36

Psalm 33:6

By the word of the LORD the heavens were made,
their starry host by the breath of his mouth.

Week Thirty-one

In the past God spoke through the prophets,
but in these last days He speaks to us through His Son.
Jesus is the radiance of His glory, the exact representation
of His being. All things are made and are
sustained by His powerful word.

Jesus suffered and died to make us holy. Now we are God's
family and Jesus is not ashamed to call us His brothers.

We are lower than angels, yet we are crowned with glory and
honor. God has put everything under our feet and will make
the world subject to us. Jesus has brought us into His glory.

ADAPTATION OF HEBREWS 1 & 2

2 Samuel 22:31

As for God, His way is perfect:
The LORD's word is flawless;
He shields all who take refuge in Him.

Week Thirty-two

God speaks of Jesus, His Son and says, "Here is my servant, whom I uphold, my chosen one in whom I delight. I put my Spirit on Him and He will bring justice to the nations.

A bruised reed He will not break, and a smoldering wick He will not snuff out. He will not falter until He establishes justice on the earth. The people will put their hope in Him."

The Lord takes us by the hand. He makes us a light to the nations; to open the eyes of the blind and set captives free. He releases from the dungeon those who sit in darkness.

ADAPTATION OF ISAIAH 42:1–7

Deuteronomy 30:14

The word is very near you;
it is in your mouth and in your heart
so you may obey it.

Week Thirty-three

Our attitude is the same as that of Christ Jesus. In every way He is God but He humbled Himself, He came to earth, took on a human likeness, and embraced the nature of a servant.

He became obedient unto death — even a criminal's death, the death of a cross. Therefore God has exalted Him to the highest place and has given Him a name above every name.

That at the name of Jesus every knee shall bow in heaven and on earth and under the earth and every tongue shall confess that Jesus is Lord, to the glory of God the Father.

ADAPTATION OF PHILIPPIANS 2:5–11

John 15:7

If you remain in Me and My words remain in you,
ask whatever you wish, and it will be done for you.

Week Thirty-four

There is no condemnation over me for I am in Christ Jesus.
The law of the Spirit of life has set me free
from the law of sin and death. God did this
by making His Son a sin offering.

The Spirit that raised Jesus from the dead now
dwells in me, therefore, He quickens my mortal body.
I am His child so I naturally desire to walk
after the Spirit and not after the flesh.

I have the Spirit of sonship in me so I cry 'Abba, Father!'
The Holy Spirit testifies with my spirit that
I am God's child and because I am His child,
I have become a co-heir with Christ.

ADAPTATION OF ROMANS 8:1–17

1 Samuel 10:6

The Spirit of the LORD will come powerfully upon you,
and you will prophesy with them;
and you will be changed into a different person.

Week Thirty-five

Jesus pours out supernatural ministry gifts by the
Holy Spirit. All who repent and believe may receive them.
The Holy Spirit gives us spiritual power under
His leading and direction.

I welcome the gifts of the Holy Spirit in my life.
I worship the Lord and obey with biblical faith,
so that I may minister. I am ready to prophesy
and give words of knowledge and wisdom.

I am here to be used by God. I avail myself
to be an instrument of healing, miracles and faith.
I will discern the spirits, speak in tongues
and interpret, as the Holy Spirit leads.

ADAPTATION OF 1 CORINTHIANS 12:1–11

John 17:17

Sanctify them by the truth; Your word is truth.

Week Thirty-six

Jesus of Nazareth was both God and man.
He performed miracles and wonders, which God
did through Him. Then, by God's design,
He was given over to wicked and evil men.

Jesus was put to death as they nailed Him to a cross,
but God raised Him from the dead.
It was impossible for death to keep Him.
Life broke through and that same life has reached me.

God raised Jesus to life and exalted Him to His right hand.
Jesus, who was crucified, is my Lord and Christ.
He saved me and gave me the gift of the Father,
His precious Holy Spirit.

ADAPTATION OF ACTS 2:22–36

Hebrews 4:12

For the word of God is alive and active.
Sharper than any double-edged sword,
it penetrates even to dividing soul and spirit,
joints and marrow;
it judges the thoughts and attitudes of the heart.

Week Thirty-seven

I offer my body as a living sacrifice, holy and pleasing
to God. This is my spiritual act of worship.
I do this in view of God's mercy,
which He extended to me when He died on the cross.

I no longer conform to the pattern of this world.
Instead, I am being transformed by the renewing of my
mind. I am being changed by the work of
the Holy Spirit who lives within me.

Therefore, I am constantly discovering God's will for my life.
As I give myself completely to Christ, I am able to find, test
and approve, God's good, pleasing and perfect will for me.

ADAPTATION OF ROMANS 12:1–2

Colossians 3:16

Let the message of Christ dwell among you richly
as you teach and admonish one another with all wisdom
through psalms, hymns, and songs from the Spirit,
singing to God with gratitude in your hearts.

Week Thirty-eight

Whoever sows sparingly will also reap sparingly;
whoever sows generously will also reap generously.
I love the Lord, therefore I give generously,
not reluctantly or under compulsion.

God loves a cheerful giver and is able to make grace abound
so that in all things, and at all times, I will have all that
I need, and I will abound in every good work.

God supplies seed to the sower and bread for food
and He will supply and increase my store of seed.
He will enlarge my harvest and make me rich
and I will be generous and thankful.

ADAPTATION OF 2 CORINTHIANS 9:6–11

Ephesians 6:17

Take the helmet of salvation
and the sword of the Spirit,
which is the word of God.

Week Thirty-nine

It is for freedom that Christ has set me free. The only thing that counts is faith expressing itself through love. I am called to freedom, but I do not use my freedom to serve a sinful nature.

With my freedom, I serve my brothers and sisters. The entire law is summed up in a single command: "Love your neighbor as yourself." I do not tear down my neighbor with my words.

I live by the Holy Spirit. The fruit of the Spirit in my life is love, joy, peace, patience, self-control, gentleness, faithfulness, goodness and kindness. The Holy Spirit is really changing me.

ADAPTATION OF GALATIANS 5:1–25

Romans 10:17

Consequently, faith comes from hearing the message, and the message is heard through the word about Christ.

Week Forty

Jesus died and rose to life again. In the same way, I will rise to life again. When Jesus appears, we who are alive and remain will follow those who have died before us.

For the Lord himself, will descend from heaven with a shout, with the voice of the archangel and the trumpet call of God. And the mystery of God will be complete, for the dead will rise.

Then we who are alive and remain will be caught up together with them in the clouds, to meet the Lord in the air, and so we shall ever be with the Lord. We shall reign with Him forever.

ADAPTATION OF 1 THESSALONIANS 4:14–17

1 Kings 8:56

Praise be to the LORD, who has given rest to
His people Israel just as He promised.
Not one word has failed of all the good promises
He gave through His servant Moses.

Week Forty-one

I humble myself under God's mighty hand,
so that He may lift me up. I cast all my cares upon Him
for He cares for me. I am not proud of myself
nor will I worry, for God watches over me.

I am on guard; I am alert and self-controlled,
for my enemy, the devil, prowls around like a roaring lion,
seeking to devour someone. I resist him steadfastly
and I stand firm in my faith.

And the God of all grace who called me
to His eternal glory will restore me and make me strong.
Even when I suffer trials, I stand firm
and continue to praise the God of my salvation.

ADAPTATION OF 1 PETER 5:6–11

Psalm 12:6

And the words of the LORD are flawless,
like silver purified in a crucible,
like gold refined seven times.

Week Forty-two

Since my youth, O God, you have taught me and to this day I declare your marvelous deeds. I declare your power to the next generation and your might to all who are to come.

Your righteousness reaches to the skies for you have done great things. There is none like you O God.
You have restored my life.
You comfort me and increase my honor once again.

I sing praises to you O my God, my lips shout for joy.
In your faithfulness you have redeemed me.
My tongue will tell of your righteous acts all day long.
You are the Holy One of Israel.

ADAPTATION OF PSALM 71:17–24

Psalm 19:14

May these words of my mouth
and this meditation of my heart
be pleasing in Your sight,
LORD, my Rock and my Redeemer.

Week Forty-three

The Lord washes away all my iniquity and cleanses me from my sin. The Lord seeks truth in my innermost being, therefore, He teaches me wisdom in the depths of my heart.

I hold my heart before the Lord and walk in righteousness. Therefore I cry, 'cleanse me with hyssop, and I will be clean; wash me and I will be whiter than snow.'

I Pray; 'Create in me a clean heart, O God and renew a right spirit within me. Restore to me the joy of my salvation and give me a willing spirit.' For God loves a humble and contrite heart.

ADAPTATION OF PSALMS 51:1–17

Psalm 33:4

For the word of the LORD is right and true;
He is faithful in all he does.

Week Forty-four

If anyone is thirsty, let him come to Jesus and drink.
I believe in Him and I am thirsty.
That is why streams of living water flow from within me.
That is the gift of the Holy Spirit.

Jesus is the light of the world. I follow Him
and I will never walk in darkness.
I have found the light of life. I am one with Jesus
and He is one with the Father who sent Him.

Because I know Jesus, I also know the Father.
Even before Abraham was born, Jesus was the great I AM.
He is my ever-present source of life and light.
All I need, I find in Him.

ADAPTATION OF JOHN 7:37–39, 8:12–58

John 6:68

Simon Peter answered him, "Lord, to whom shall we go? You have the words of eternal life.

❦ Week Forty-five ❧

I declare the word of God concerning Israel.
When all the nations rise up against her,
God will make Jerusalem an immovable rock.
All, who attack her, will injure themselves.

Then, the leaders of Judah will be like a torch among
sheaves. They will say, 'We are strong for God is with us.'
They will consume the surrounding peoples,
but Jerusalem shall remain.

Then, the Lord shall destroy the nations that attack
Jerusalem. And the people of Israel will look on
Him whom they have pierced, and the Lord
will cleanse them from sin and impurity.

ADAPTATION OF ZECHARIAH 12:1–13, 13:

Psalm 119:103

How sweet are Your words to my taste,
sweeter than honey to my mouth!

Week Forty-six

I declare the word of the Lord. He will gather all nations to the valley of Jehoshaphat. He will judge the nations because they scattered and abused Israel and divided His land.

Then, multitudes will be in the valley of decision.
For the day of the Lord will come.
The Lord will roar from Zion and thunder
from Jerusalem and the earth and sky will tremble.

At that time, the Lord will be a refuge for His people.
The Lord will dwell with His people and
He will pardon them and a fountain of life
will flow from the house of the Lord forever.

ADAPTATION OF JOEL 3:1–21

John 1:23

John replied in the words of Isaiah the prophet,
"I am the voice of one calling in the wilderness,
'Make straight the way for the Lord'"

Week Forty-seven

I join in to sing the song of Moses and the song of the Lamb.
'Great and marvelous are your deeds, Lord God Almighty.
Just and true are your ways, King of the ages.

Who will not fear you, O Lord, and bring glory
to your name? For you alone are holy.
All nations will come and worship before you,
for your righteous acts have been revealed.'

The temple in heaven will open. It is filled with God's glory.
And I will join the sea of glass and be victorious
over the devil. I will receive a harp from God
and sing with the holy choir.

ADAPTATION OF REVELATION 15:3–21

Acts 19:20

In this way the word of the Lord
spread widely and grew in power.

Week Forty-eight

I have confidence to enter the holy place by the blood
of Jesus, by a new and living way opened for me
through the curtain. The curtain is Christ's body
that was crucified for my salvation.

Jesus is my Great High Priest. He is over the house of God.
I draw near to God through Him.
I have a sincere heart and full assurance of faith for
He cleansed me of a guilty conscience.

The one who has promised me life, is faithful.
So, I encourage others in the love of God.
I spur them on to good deeds and remind them
to meet together regularly with God's people.

ADAPTATION OF HEBREWS 10:19–25

Psalm 130:5

I wait for the LORD, my whole being waits,
and in His word I put my hope.

Week Forty-nine

I put my trust in God so that trouble will not rule in my heart. In my Father's family there are many places.
I give everything to Him for He has prepared a place for me.

Jesus has gone ahead of me into the presence of the Father.
One day, He will come back and take me to be with Him.
He and the Father are one and now, I am one with them.

Jesus is the way, the truth and the life.
No one comes to the Father but through Him.
Because He lives in me, I may ask anything in His name, according to His will, and He will do it.

ADAPTATION OF JOHN 14:1–14

Psalm 89:1

I will sing of the LORD's great love forever;
with my mouth I will make Your faithfulness
known through all generations.

Week Fifty

Jesus is the vine and God is the gardener. I am one of His branches. I thank God for pruning me so that I can be more fruitful. I remain in Christ for that is how I bear good fruit.

Apart from the Lord, I can do nothing.
As I abide in Him and His words abide in me,
I ask whatever I wish and it is given to me. This is for
the glory of the Father and not for my glory.

Jesus and the Father love me, so I will remain in His love.
I am filled with joy and my joy is complete.
The love I have from God overflows to others,
for He has chosen me to bear fruit.

ADAPTATION OF JOHN 15:1–12

John 7:38

Whoever believes in Me, as Scripture has said,
rivers of living water will flow from within them.

❦ Week Fifty-one ❦

I will give thanks to the Lord for He is good;
His love endures forever. In my anguish I cried
to the Lord and He answered by setting me free.
The Lord is with me; I will not be afraid.

The Lord is my strength and my song;
He has become my salvation.
Shouts of joy and victory resound in the tents of the
righteous; the Lord's right hand has done mighty things.

This is the day the Lord has made;
I will rejoice and be glad in it.
The Lord has made His light shine on me.
So, I join in the festive procession
up to the house of the Lord. I praise Him.

ADAPTATION OF PSALM 118:1–29

Revelation 12:11

They triumphed over him (the devil)
by the blood of the Lamb
and by the word of their testimony.

Week Fifty-two

The river of life flows from the throne of God.
The tree of life yields its fruit every month,
and the leaves of the tree are for the healing of the nations.
Soon, there will be no more curse.

The throne of God and of the Lamb will be in the city;
I will serve Him for I am His servant.
I will see His face and His name will be on my forehead.
I will reign with Him forever.

Behold the Lord is coming. The Spirit and the bride
say "Come!" He is the Alpha and the Omega.
I hear His call and drink from the river of Life.
The grace of the Lord is covering me.

ADAPTATION OF REVELATION 22:1–21

www.ingramcontent.com/pod-product-compliance
Lightning Source LLC
Chambersburg PA
CBHW010449010526
44118CB00019B/2517